RED SUMMER

RED SUMMER

by Amaud Jamaul Johnson

TUPELO PRESS

First paperback edition April 2006

Tupelo Press
PO Box 539, Dorset, Vermont 05251
802.366.8185 • Fax 802.362.1883
editor@tupelopress.org • web www.tupelopress.org

Cover art: *Yesterday*, assemblage, by Daniel LaRue Johnson
Cover and text designed by William Kuch, WK Graphic Design

For Cherene

Acknowledgments

Grateful acknowledgement is made to the editors of the following journals, in which versions of these poems originally appeared:

From the Fishouse: "Burlesque," "The Lost Sea," "Portion Given," "On This Side of Mercy," "The Manassa Mauler," "Junior Goes Home"

Gathering Ground: "Spirit of the Dead Watching"

New England Review: "Names we sing in sleep & anger"

Poetry Daily: "Names we sing in sleep & anger"

Rivendell: "The Collection of Stone"

The Virginia Quarterly Review: "The Maple Remains," "Chicago Citizen Testifies in His Defense," "Elaine, 1919," "Big City."

For financial support, criticism, and community:
The Creative Writing Program at the University of Wisconsin-Madison, The Wallace Stegner Fellowship Program at Stanford University, The Cave Canem Foundation, The Hurston/Wright Foundation, and The Bread Loaf Writers Conference.

For your support as colleagues:
Ronald Wallace, Jesse Lee Kercheval, Amy Quan Barry, Judy Mitchell, Ron Kuka, Rob Nixon, Lorrie Moore, and Roberta Hill.

For your guidance and encouragement:
Toi Derricotte, Cornelius Eady, Carolyn Micklem, Sarah Micklem, Elizabeth Alexander, Tim Seibles, Nikky Finney, Marita Golden, Edward Hirsch, Michael Collier, Devon Jersild, Noreen Cargill, Angela Jackson, Kenneth A. McClane, Mark A. Sanders and Eavan Boland.

For your friendship, suggestions, and support:
Douglas Kearney, Camille Dungy, Tyehimba Jess, Quraysh Ali Lansana, A. Van Jordan, Bruce Snider, Shara Lessley, Emily Rosko, Brian Spears, Geoff Brock, Robin Ekiss, Monica Ferrel, John Lundberg, David Roderick, K. Bradford, Roger Sedarat, Pablo Peschiera, G.C. Waldrop, and Tony Michels.

For your faith in my work:
Carl Phillips

For your honesty and love:
Cherene, Hayden, and my family

CONTENTS

Names We Sing in Sleep & Anger

Part One

3······The Maple Remains
4······The Manassa Mauler
5······Chicago Citizen Testifies in His Defense
6······On Loving Red
7······Big City
8······The Classifieds
9······Junior Goes Home
10······Elaine, 1919

Part Two

17······The Lost Sea
18······Burlesque
19······Aesthetics
20······Stones River
21······Taffy Pull
22······Of Shadows and Wisteria
24······Rumor
25······Getting Along
26······Bones for My Bread
27······On This Side of Mercy
28······End of Summer
29······Space Travel
30······Watching a Plane Crash
31······Sunday Dinner

Part Three

35······Spirit of the Dead Watching
36······to trouble water

37······Portion Given
38······A Fear of Thunder
40······On Being Good Men
41······Greenwood
42······Buffalo Creek
43······Liturgy for Joshua
44······Why Bryant Gumbel Will Never Apologize
45······The Juice
46······The Gunfighter
47······The Sense of Unspoken Things
48······Elegy
49······Prayer for a Practical God
50······The Collection of Stone
51······The Gospel of Accord
52······Culture
53······Hayden

54······Notes

NAMES WE SING IN SLEEP & ANGER

Like fishermen at dusk, the soldiers returned
from war with stories slumped over their shoulders;
their fingers firm at the knot, the netting, thick
and tangled with the names of the dead.

None could explain how the flood of life all around
them escaped like water from between cupped hands,
how the bodies of men they loved began to crust
the earth like salt, how destruction danced slapdash
and unashamed everywhere, and still they survived.

When I came home from college proud, my educated
mouth agape, a tackle box of words, slick and glossy
and I saw the names of my friends, the young men
I fought with, learned to drink with, and left behind

Lil' Rocc, Pumpkin, Ulysses, Junebug, Aghoster
names spray-painted throughout our neighborhood
in memoriam, I couldn't understand how a god
could make one life possible and strip the world
clean of so many, or how, like high-watermarks
the dead remind the living of the coming of storms.

Part One

"It never looked as terrible as it was and it made her wonder if hell was a pretty place too. Fire and brimstone all right, but hidden in lacy groves...the sycamores beat out the children every time."

—Toni Morrison, *Beloved*

THE MAPLE REMAINS

Vicksburg, Mississippi
May 16, 1919

For the general good
Such, even the smell
Is customary; like figs
Gray and gamy, rotting
Among the orchard mulch.

And an old woman
Remembers her children
As little monkeys for its branches,
Their hinged arms and legs are
Indistinguishable at dusk.

She remembers the clearing
When she and her husband
First arrived in Vicksburg;
How Charles leaned against
The trunk, his face washed
With shadow and smoke;

How he looked at the land
The crest and its antiseptic
Slopes and said "this is home."

The old woman remembers
And pleads for its felling
And a young man gazing
Among the throngs responds:

"What was done here
Last night, was done
For you and for every
Woman and for every
Girl in Warren County."

THE MANASSA MAULER

(July 4, 1919)

The peach of Willard's face
split wide, ran sweet
and sticky on Dempsey's gloves.
Canvas met the lumbering
burden of his body
seven times.

By the end of the first,
blood, sweat and saliva
pooled at their feet, swirled like
dashes of hot sauce in a bucket
of egg whites, fell first in drops
then by the drum.

Across a field of straw
hats and seersucker suits,
Toledo's finest, wet with
Willard's insides. One woman,

genteel in dress, leaned forward
with her lace handkerchief
and asked the referee for a tooth.

Dempsey's now freckled face,
calm and careful as a butcher's
before the final chop.

CHICAGO CITIZEN TESTIFIES IN HIS DEFENSE

July 27th, 1919: Eugene Williams, 17, found dead at the 26th Street Beach, who apparently drowned after being struck on the head by a blunt object.

What might seem like dumb luck
isn't, it's not happenstance, or being
in the wrong place at the right time,
it's about learning to see a certain point
in the air, and wanting to touch it
with the stone. What I know about
religion, I know what the sky calls
from your hand, you deliver. I know
the angle of ascent, the pitch and point
of the line, and I'm not ashamed.
The fate of the rock, like that of the boy,
falls somewhere between gravity and god.

ON LOVING RED

After her divorce
The first thing my mother
Bought was a Firebird;
Candy apple with a phoenix

Spread-eagled on the hood,
The words "Formula One"
In two-tone racing stripes
Along the sides.

My stepfather drove an olive
Toronado. He had a habit of hitting
Stray dogs in our neighborhood;
Three by my count, and one

So big it dented the grill
And bloodied his windshield.
He walked the hallways
Of our house that way

Reckless and always ready
To run somebody down.
Sometimes, I wonder how many
Miles we tiptoed in those years.

BIG CITY

He promises a canary dress, white gloves,
says they'll eat chops, thick as her thighs,
that they'll order doubles of the "finest,"
see all the Big Names when they arrive.
But it's the thought of them dead:
half of what they own draped around them,
her head against his chest, his back slack
against the headboard, all their letters unopened,
bills not paid, long knocks, the notices tacked
outside their door. It's not knowing
whether some smell would introduce them
to their neighbors or a landlord wheeling
them out into the hallway; the highboy
he chipped on the drive up, the silver
she inherited from her mother, her hatboxes,
stacked high next to them like a wedding cake
waiting to be buried. He heard that "up there"
the wind had talons sharp enough to hook
a grown man beneath his collarbone and carry
him a full city block. He heard that you learned
the months by measuring the length of their shadows
and even summer was like a quality of night.

THE CLASSIFIEDS

Boy

Needs Negro, honest
Good with hands, strong back (a must)
Steady position

Elevator

High class apartment
Illustrious clientele
A chance to move up

Porter

Experienced man
Generally useful for
Brooklyn family

College

Needs educated
Colored grad, best references
Must return to South

JUNIOR GOES HOME

(for my grandfather)

When Junior returned to Texas
The sky caravaned down behind
Him, narrow as the fishing creeks
He often described in his stories.

He spoke of those who wouldn't leave,
Women who thought California
Was too far, that we'd be sliced
And swallowed whole by the ocean.

He spoke of men who couldn't trade
Cotton and cattle for steel; couldn't
Leave home, this family, this history.

Our reunions are pecan smoked
Meats and boiling crawfish
Brought fresh from Galveston,
Where the Gulf is dark as roux.

And Cousin Melvin saying, "it's good
To see good people on good occasions"
The shirtsleeve of his half-arm
Pinned like the flap of an envelope.

And we ate the sweetbreads, our lips
And chins stained red as guilt.

Junior took off his shoes and socks
His brown feet, creased as parchment
Buried deep in the dark grass.

ELAINE, 1919

(1)

four men, businessmen, down
coon hunting from Helena;
two Fisk men, two Philander,
cussing over old football scores,
humming fight songs, crouched
behind a late-autumn thicket.

on the way back to their Packard,
coonskin full in their sacks,
their bellies full of corn liquor.
and some friends, smiling friends said:

>   *had some trouble round these parts,*
>   *aint safe for y'all to be drivin,*
>   *you boys better off takin the train.*

and when the train was stopped,
their flaccid bodies, like golden calves,
were tossed hand to hand above
a sea of flame-lit grinning faces.
the last alive strained, sweat

and blood in his eyes, to see
his folk, and maybe those friends
as he too was washed away in waves
of human darkness.

(2)

wind whispers its prayer
through turning trees, exposing
branch bark like weathered black skin.
wind whispers a voiceless laughter,
echoes of children, lost love and secrets.
an indian summer haunting
this october, haunting
this air expectant.

air, amber at dusk.
amber cabin-light distant
where families struggle to give thanks.
this bitter harvest of bad memories
and broken promises.
bitter harvest as night
and new moon come coffee black,
wind whispering still to heavens.

(3)

pack combs the canebreak,
beating for bodies. and hounds,
hydra-headed with wet
noses, sniff the stench. rank,
the whoop, hoot and holler
of dog days and men.

papers say:

NEGRO DESPERADOS PLAN
MASSACRE, WHITES TAKE ARMS

WHITES OUTSIDE HOOP SPUR, ARKANSAS
UNCOVER GET-RICH QUICK SCHEME

NEGRO "PAUL REVERES" RIDE,
CALL TO KILL ALL WHITE SOUTHERNERS

and thus, the crow's meat was served.
flightless birds for bloated black
bellies brandish their priggish
swagger along the highway.
smoke thick as nail-clippings
still curling in the morning air.

(4)

truth be told:
        some words can barely be
thought.
        some can't be spoken above a
whisper.

that first night, those few
men, farmers all, huddled
in the hollow of their church
and someone let fall "union."

        black dead are numbered.
        white dead are named.

Clinton Lee was first
to fall and the call went
from Macon to Milwaukee.
the bloodletting lasted three
days and the court cases,
less than three hours

so only stumps and stubble
of men remain; works done, wishes
undone all lay waste among the rubble.

Part Two

"The example would be all the more powerful if we got the wrong one."
—Charles W. Chesnutt,
The Marrow of Tradition

THE LOST SEA

For generations, hillbillies stumbled
into the hollow of the rock, testing

themselves against the hard darkness
treacherous as the mouth of a dead man.

Below ground, alcohol echoes in every chamber
of the heart, so the bootleggers moved in,

and plenty a man, lost in the pleasures of his work,
blew himself from this kingdom and the next.

They called it the curse of Chief Craighead,
how the Confederates, mining for saltpeter,

and the mushroom farmers disappeared.
Lovers, searching for the forgiveness of shadows,

found years later in dry heaps like jaguar bones.
In 1905, a thirteen year old, named Ben Sands,

slipped seventy yards in a sinkhole, and claimed
he hit standing water. It took fifty years before

they found the lake, fifteen acres across
and over eighty feet deep, stalactites still dripping,

anthodite in full bloom across the cavern walls.
Locals called the big one "Betsy the Milking Cow"

and this became the talk of Sweetwater, all the talk
of East Tennessee: how a boy unearthed a lake

and grew old a liar; how the truth of the rock,
the fluidity of darkness, became the truth of the soul.

BURLESQUE

Watch the fire undress him,
how flame fingers each button,
rolls back his collar, unzips him
without sweet talk or mystery.

See how the skin begins to gather
at his ankles, how it slips into
the embers, how it shimmers
beneath him, unshapen, iridescent

as candlelight on a dark negligee.
Come, look at him, at all his goods,
how his whole body becomes song,
an aria of light, a psalm's kaleidoscope.

Listen as he lets loose an opus,
night's national anthem, the tune
you can't name, but can't stop humming.
There, he burns brilliant as a blue note.

AESTHETICS

we must know a force
greater than our weaknesses
—Jean Toomer

like most boys, ignorant
or fearful of beauty, we
pinned back the wings

of butterflies and plucked
off their legs, and watched
and watched them tumble

from leaves like pinecones
wheeling from rooftops;
and we laughed.

we crumbled alka-seltzer
for the pigeons, "those
flying rats" my mother's

ex-husband once called.
their bodies floundering like
toys flung from a window.

white foam from their mouths
stark against the asphalt
framing their artless convulsions

and we laughed
with open-mouths until
tears dripped from our

chins and our throats
were raw with the rightness
of god.

STONES RIVER

The battlefield of my grandfather's face
had no memorial, it was a place no historian
took the time to study, a site few would know,
but we went there often, sat in the quiet
of his room, and stared across the shattered
landscape of his smile. We were long from
the night when the line was drawn, when
one side of his body took issue with the other
and decided to secede, stumbling off into a dark
and silent fury. Thinking of him still, I see
only the pupil of his right eye, how it hung,
listless, snarled in the barbed-white of his iris;
his cheek and jaw, jumbled like sandbags
too heavy to be restacked; and his chin, sunken,
half-buried in the rolling fat of his neck.
No matter how much my mother talked about him,
about who he was, the figure of a man he cut,
I'd try, but I just couldn't remember him whole.

TAFFY PULL

after the rush
           and wind
of southern sport

      the sampling
and pickling
          of parts
for souvenirs

          an ear here
a toe, a tooth wrapped
      in napkins
with care

      carnival of flesh
pink and tender
          as cotton candy

children dance round
      the fire with fistfuls

smoldering sticks, clasped
          like sparklers

tracing an old alphabet
          in the night sky

OF SHADOWS AND WISTERIA

Growing up, when Papa talked
About their trips cross country,
All seven of them jam-packed
Into his light blue '62 Bonneville,

Half-full meant empty, sunset
Could mean speed up or slow
Down, depending on the county,
Fourteen was good enough to help

Drive, and if you ate too much
Too soon, it meant you went hungry.
One summer, he said, they couldn't
Get the ragtop back up, so they

Bought straw hats in San Antonio,
Rolled up the windows and moved on.
Boy, you don't know how good you got it.
Let's blame it on the literary South.

Maybe it was the illusion of charm,
The idea of hospitality, a wistfulness
For Spanish moss and wisteria, but
I shouldn't have been caught off guard

When a man in a Waffle House parking lot
Glared down at me from his pickup truck
And mouthed a word I couldn't make out.
What I saw in his eyes was something

Like love; his eyes tethered to that same
Space in the body, bound to what waits
There, this other inhabitant, what fans
The spirit like blood meal and feeds.

And this was the first time anyone had looked
Into me and stared as if he knew some truth,
Some lesson I'd forgotten or hadn't learned.

rumor

is

a toothless

tiger

it gums

its prey

to boredom

leaves

it alone

to rot

in mid

summer

sun

GETTING ALONG

While night dreams   day won't
Forget so the morning with Christmas'
Magic and we hurried on our clothes
Scuttling from bed to door to front door
Wistful of what the darkness had brought.

The night no sirens blew and
If it was an earthquake the
Doorframes and tabletops made do
But for the screaming the jeers & cheers
Of fight flight and fantasy we
Were ill prepared.

Masses stark at daybreak as the night
Before with fistfuls   and
Cars ramming security gates fish
Chicken and milk from the market.
Distinctly a boy outside Blockbuster   I
Remember "free video rentals" he said.

This shoe an empty beer bottle and
One woman's earring are trophies.
We watched poor Rodney   the 3rd day,
Carted out in front of the cameras
Even his face fully healed seemed
As puffed and swollen as Emmett Till's.

His face and we wondered if
After all this if he understood
What Helen felt as the city burned.

BONES FOR MY BREAD

There is always a woman,
Janus-faced, half hidden
behind a curtain, peering
from her bedroom window.

There is always a crowd
halfcocked, coal oil handy
needful of some gesture,
an outcry, or an epithet

something to make what
they have already decided
easier. Word of an outrage
catches, spreads like wildfire.

Turns a Sunday picnic
into a parade, turns
a parade into a pilgrimage.

ON THIS SIDE OF MERCY

after Mississippi John Hurt

Some nights, I need to feel like the Sheriff's backstage
And a too-tough niggah, who I owe more money than what's
In my pocket, is standing out front, and I know my ass
Is too drunk or too slow to make the exit and keep my guitar.
When I close my eyes and palm the soundboard,
My fingers make a constellation, and my mind is all about
The last time with my woman; her nails strumming
My ribcage, how her name tastes, hovering in my mouth
Like a circle of smoke. Then the cry I let go, like a bird
Perched on my tongue. Then each chord, a new vein opening.
And then I don't give a damn about nothing, anymore.

END OF SUMMER

Night soup of fireflies,
Dancing among the azaleas;
The muted roar of snapdragons
Wakes the dead.

The mourning moon
Light in the honeyed dew
Drops, crusting a green
Still universe.

September sunrise,
This golden, bolder
Separating Georgia pine
Rolling over the distance.

And the clatter of school
Children, piercing the silence.
Their laughter, sweet as lemon
Drops, as cool as peppermint.

SPACE TRAVEL

After we'd housed enough candy,
and had entertained ourselves
again with the possibility of ruin,
we circled the skyrocket
that hovered before the Big D,
and sifted for change between
the drunks and Jehovah's Witnesses.

That night, like something spit up
then poured from a dirty glass;
that night when we noticed the moon,
its fractured light gleaming among
the seasons of green bottle glass,
and knew no matter how late we stayed,
no one would come searching.

One by one, we mounted the rocket,
wedged our new adolescence
into its painted gun-metal cockpit
and counted down: *five, four, three,*
two, one, and nothing changed.
We were trapped somewhere between
moondust and the bottom of a fish bowl.

WATCHING A PLANE CRASH

You won't remember who died,
or how many, or whether the shirt
you wore, you borrowed from your brother;
not the last word, not the expression
on the face of the man next to you,
whether you reached for his hand first,
how his touch might have made the cold
splinter in your palm. Light comes, then heat,
then the weight of sound rushing.

And you will turn, as if before sleeping
you'd forgotten to pull the shade, and at dawn
the sun reached you, as might a lover, with whom
you'd argued the night before, and slept in anger,
your dreams stitched by what you could have said,
and come morning, her hand pulls at your shoulder,
and you turn to consider the possibilities.

SUNDAY DINNER

Our arms dangled
Like streamers webbed
Between the beams
Of an abandoned dancehall.

My oldest uncle, sweating
His afternoon drink through
His dress shirt, stumbled
Through the blessing.

Merciful Father...Great Redeemer
And the grandbabies blinked
With each pause, always unsure
When or whether to open their eyes.

We straddled the quiet
Of each empty chair, those
Fissures of death's dinner table,
With small talk and laughter.

Part Three

"To write a blues song
is to regiment riots
and pluck gems from graves."
        —Etheridge Knight, "Haiku"

SPIRIT OF THE DEAD WATCHING

"Men are apt to idolize or fear that which they cannot understand, especially if it be a woman."
—Jean Toomer

Like so many stones, a handful
of jasper or black opal scattered
along the banks of the Papenoo,

Gauguin has fixed his eye upon
a native girl working among the women.
She twists and beats the wash dry

for her mother, readying the bundles
to be carried back to their village,
and Gauguin is in love again.

Long from those indifferent hours,
long from the doors of the *Maison du jouir*
and the affected gaze of his mistresses.

In this paradise, all of his desires
collapse into color, become baskets
of guava, plantain, and avocado.

Tonight, he will offer her chocolate
and hold a red silk scarf before the fire.
Beneath banyan, palm, and sweet gum,

he will try to divine the body's secret,
unburden himself of the thought of history
and paint his language into their silences.

to trouble water

flat stones skipping dark
water ring. your nipples sail
like monet's lilies.

PORTION GIVEN

Halve the heart-

Set the meat aside
In slivers

From the fatty part
That loves him.

Mother,
You've always been good

About whipping something
Up from nothing.

Even memory,
The bits skewered,

Speech sifting, words measured
By the quarter cup.

Give it time, Son.
Low heat. Slow cook.

Even when I thought
He might kill you.

Even after he changed
The locks.

I don't want to hear
How it might have ended.

Let's strain the blood from gristle.
Let's crack the window-

And leave the scraps for the dog.

A FEAR OF THUNDER

Last night, I heard a woman crying,

And her voice grew thick with each hour.

————

At first, I thought, two voices:

Lovers, or maybe an old couple,

A husband stumbling home,

A wife, made tired by excuses.

————

What part has been torn open?

————

Nights my mother didn't sleep

And mornings we threw clothes

Across the yard, and I learned

To manage the weight of a gun.

————

How the crying rose to every window,

Pulsed, it seemed,

Until the darkness began to clot,

And it was impossible

For anyone awake, anyone within her reach,

To breathe and not drink of her sorrow.

———

Summer, when it stormed hard,

My mother turned off everything,

Covered the mirrors, and we sat

Listening to the Devil beat his wife.

———

Where is this flesh unstrung?

———

And that cry seemed to claw

From her body, not her throat,

Nor anyplace ever made for singing.

———

Of this pain, what women

Know, her cry seemed carved

Of muscle and soft bone.

ON BEING GOOD MEN

(for Damian)

Because you were a good man,
And we had spent so much
Of our adolescence thinking about
Being good men, about being better
Than our fathers, about proving
The world wrong, that black men
Could love, that we could be true
To our wives, strong for our children

Because so much had come to pass
How the narcotic night called us
How the streets beneath us ached
From sorrow and we survived

When you said you understood
What made men leave, how you stood
In the doorway, your wife and kids
Asleep, your keys like a knife
At your wrist, how you heard your
Name echo in the chorus of darkness
And were not afraid

Because you were a good man
And I had spent so much of my life
Trying to be a good man too
I could see your truth, like all
The truths who turned their backs
On us, the men who jumped
Freight trains, the men who drove
For milk and never looked back

How we run from ourselves
From the chaos of our hearts
From our inability to witness
Our failures in those we love

GREENWOOD

The ash adrift
like a bevy of black
butterflies

The morning fires
frolic from house to church
and school as carefree
as children at play

And the body crops
are planted with the precision
of sweet corn and okra

BUFFALO CREEK

Logan County, West Virginia
February 26, 1972

Before the houses began to list,

before they went careening, barreling
        headlong to splinter against railroad trestles
              and before the bulkheads snapped,

scattering debris and bodies a quarter-mile
        across a slick and weather-stripped landscape,

you could see them, still at their windows—

        each eye, hurried; each face, dark and motionless
           as an inlet. Men, who had chipped

and chiseled years from their lives,
        a darker atmosphere looming in their chests,
           drowned in their beds with their families.

Twice buried. Once without ceremony
        then again after the sediment settled
           and all the math was done.

What does it mean to wake to the roar of shadows,
        to watch your life bubble up beneath you
           and wait to see it seep

underneath your bedroom door?
        When do you know that everything, everything

around you has become a disaster?

LITURGY FOR JOSHUA

Seven days you'll walk these walls,
And you'll gather seven priests
To carry seven trumpets,
And for six days you'll circle

The city once. Seven priests
Shall bear before the ark, sound
Their trumpets. And you'll circle
These walls on the seventh day

Seven times. The priests will sound
Their trumpets, the men will shout;
These walls, on the seventh day,
Will fall. So Joshua takes

The good news to the men, shouts:
"For the Lord hath given you
The city." Joshua takes
His message before the priests

"For the Lord hath given you…"
The next morning they circle:
The armed guard, the ark, the priests.
On faith they round the city.

For five more days they circle,
Each day like the one before.
On faith they round the city.
And the priests blow their trumpets,

Each day like the one before.
Seven days these walls they walk,
Priests, again, blow their trumpets,
Men shout, and all tumbles down.

WHY BRYANT GUMBEL WILL NEVER APOLOGIZE

This night abandons my lover's back
as ocean from the hump of a white whale.

This is the jewel of her skin, and this my hand upon her.

And this rush of history between my legs;
a love full, over-grown as life, stolen from a melon patch.

When I was a boy, when this world seemed simple,
I wrote Darla love letters, imagined the flip of her hair

soft against my cheek; us giggling as we zoomed through
neighborhoods, black and white in my soapbox racer.

Never again will I live a life limited to peepholes.

Alfalfa and Spanky are gone, and now my breath is hot,
desperate as a field hand's just called up to the Big House,

revenge on my tongue, thick and heavy as the taste of her.

Maybe my wife will understand. Maybe my children will learn
the secret lives of their heroes, see beneath the mask, under those

tight red and blue panties. Whatever the case, whatever you
might think, after this I can never wear that bow-tie again.

THE JUICE

greasy good morning

sweet inky tendrils
swollen & sticky
soldered to neck
like fat earthworms
tender on asphalt

night's slick sleep:
the slippery pillows
& plastic bags

globs of glycerin, caked
in crevices like snot

& still
I loved my curl

with whips of wonder
on my shoulders,
I felt ready for the world

the curl changed
everything

first, for folks who
couldn't grow their natural
long enough

then the shag. grown men
big, black as jack johnson
with pink & green rollers
ablaze like neon lights

& me at 14, before I knew any better;
this conditioned love was unconditional

& carefree

THE GUNFIGHTER

(for Amy)

Thirty five years
and I ain't even got
a good watch.

It ends how it begins
in smoke and dust.
Just the want of a piece

of something soft:
scraps of brushed leather
or a fist of rabbit fur

or a woman. Trouble
is cheap and plenty.
Never enough time

for a proper wash.
Men bring me their
bodies and I lay them

down, gently; baptize them
like a priest in a river of blood.
I am who they know before God.

THE SENSE OF UNSPOKEN THINGS

there is still   still inside—
not dead,   but waiting
           and aware of life;
           is sweet as almond
           and hibiscus are distinct.

quicken in the quiet
that is my spirit.
engaged in what first
man had—
the joy of wind
on my face, sun
at my feet, dancing.

           estranged evolution... but
           these moments—bitter
           and sweet—are
           eternal.

ELEGY

(for sean)

impossible air.
light peeled from the guttersnipe's
underbelly. everything i love
suffocates, perfectly.

maybe if we all leap
into the tar pits, arms cuffed
and eyes open, we'll be exhumed
black and precious as a dream
woven underwater.

PRAYER FOR A PRACTICAL GOD

I've seen a man drown
In an inch of imagination

I've seen men buried alive
Neck-deep in sunlight

Lord, I aint askin for mountains
But I need somethin to move

This earth inside me
Or someone to seed my soul

THE COLLECTION OF STONE

(for William Meredith)

the great poet, the dying man
says that he will stand & read

his mouth now a quarry
of words, full of chipped & angled

sound. we gather handfuls
& rush what will not spill

into the pockets of memory
hallie & laurel beside me

somewhere between the beginning
of what will become our lives

& this man, this poet
this life before us of believing

in what words can do
& i ask how will we be loved

who will hold us, wipe our mouths
& help with the lines we've missed

or misread. in the end, who will listen
& help with the collection of stone

THE GOSPEL OF ACCORD

I built a bone temple

I made my mind
a scaffolding and spent
the better part

of a decade on my back
painting you across
the ceiling of my skull

Ushering a congregation
of women into my body
I spoke only in tongues

whispered night song
into the altar of their mouths
and found none possessed

I tried to hollow my spirit
of want and scrape memory
from my brain's bowl

Still, like some bedeviled light
casting its shadow play along
the walls of my imagination

you kept coming back to me

CULTURE

Ellison fed me
yams, piping hot
wrapped in tinfoil
with butter dripping
from the corners
and he dared
me to eat
them in public.

HAYDEN

What did I know, what did I know
Of gazing silences and terrored stone

Brilliances; beauty of what's hardbitten
The auroral darkness which is God

Then you arrived, meditative, ironic
My head gripped in bony vice

Mouth of agony shaping a cry it cannot utter
What did I know, what did I know

Of a changing permanence
The stains and dirty tools of struggle

Weaving a wish and a weariness together
Years before your time. Years and years

I gaze through layered light
Within the rock of the undiscovered suns

I see, I walk with you among
The landscape lush, metallic, flayed

Behind us, beyond us now
The very sunlight here seems flammable

Notes

In "Names we sing in sleep & anger," the title is taken from Yusef Komunyakaa's "Missing in Action," first published in *Dien Cai Dau*.

In "The Classifieds," some phrases are excerpts published in the classified sections of *The New York Age* and *The Chicago Defender* during the summer of 1919.

In "The Maple Remains," the last stanza quotes a witness of the murder of Lloyd Clay, published by the NAACP in *Thirty Years of Lynching in the United States, 1921-1946*.

In "Elaine, 1919," the headlines in the third section reference "The Elaine Riot Project," newspaper clippings collected at Arkansas State University by Dr. Sarah Wilkerson-Freeman.

In "Aesthetics," the epigraph is an aphorism from Jean Toomer's *Essentials*.

In "Spirit of the Dead Watching," the epigraph is from Toomer's short story, "Fern."

In "The Gunfighter," the first stanza is a quote from *The Gunfighter* (1950), a film staring Gregory Peck; directed by Henry King.

"Hayden" is a cento. Each line is taken from Robert Hayden's *Collected Poems*, edited by Frederick Glaysher.